C000006775

writing in multilingual classrooms

Viv Edwards

Reading and Language Information Centre
University of Reading

For Mary Martyn-Johns, with thanks

Acknowledgments

I am very grateful to the children and teachers who provided me with examples of writing for this book and, in particular, to Katherine Forster, Naomi Froy, Sally Garforth and Elizabeth Pye of Redlands Primary School; Sheila Egan and Ruth Cummin of St Jude's First and Middle School; Sarah Green; and Elena Mauro and Monica Forty of Bangha Bundhu School. Warm thanks to Angela Redfern and Prue Goodwin for reading and commenting on drafts. Finally, I would like to acknowledge the permission given by Hounslow Language Service to reproduce the Urdu overlay from the Elmtree Farm *Scenario* program on page 12 and the page from *The hare and the tortoise* on page 20, and to *Languages Matter* for permission to reproduce the example of children's writing on page 26.

Meeting the needs of bilingual pupils

This book is part of a series of training materials which consists of three separate packs:
• *Reading in multilingual classrooms*
• *Writing in multilingual classrooms*
• *Speaking and listening in multilingual classrooms*

Each pack comprises:
• a course leader's handbook
• overhead transparencies
• a teacher's book

The teacher's books are also available separately.

Publications of related interest

Other titles from the Reading and Language Information Centre of interest to teachers in multilingual classrooms include:

Building bridges: multilingual resources for children
Multilingual Resources for Children Project

The AIMER Year Book
Annually updated lists of anti-racist, multicultural teaching materials to support all areas of the curriculum, as well as community language teaching and language support teaching

The multicultural guide to children's literature 0–12
Edited by Rosemary Stones

Working with parents
Penny Kenway

© Viv Edwards 1995
ISBN 0 7049 0772 0

Published by
Reading and Language Information Centre
University of Reading
Bulmershe Court
Earley
Reading RG6 1HY

Contents

Introduction

Schools in many parts of the world now serve multilingual populations. Children arrive with a range of experience of the written word. Some are already proficient readers and writers; others may be experiencing formal education for the first time. Teachers are sometimes unclear about the best approach to children in the process of learning a second language, and have often had few opportunities for training in this area.

The main focus of this book is on practical strategies which help children to develop as writers. The activities which support bilingual pupils are, in most cases, the same as those which work for native speakers. The organization, materials and ideas which are successful with groups of English speaking children will also work well in multilingual classrooms.

A range of issues will be explored, including

- the writing process
- approaches to the teaching of writing
- ways of supporting children's development as writers
- the use of other languages in writing to the benefit of both monolingual and bilingual children
- the secretarial skills of writing
- assessment.

The writing process

The traditional view of writing was that children needed to be taught a complex set of skills in strict sequence. Writing was seen primarily in terms of visual perception, small motor control and hand-eye coordination. Children were expected to spend a great deal of time practising their writing skills: copying handwriting patterns, forming letters, writing words, then sentences and paragraphs with the appropriate punctuation. Decontextualized exercises were used to drill children in the requisite skills.

The research findings of recent years, however, point to a very different picture of what is involved in becoming a successful writer. Children are now seen as active rather than passive participants, interacting with and using language to construct meaning for themselves and others. Investigations of children's writing at home (eg Bissex 1980) and at school (eg Graves 1983; Calkins 1983) have focussed on what precisely happens when children write; the many functions of writing; and the developmental process as children's control over the written word grows. Current thinking in this area can be summarised as follows:

- Reading, writing, speaking and listening are inter related – and not discrete – language skills. All four language skills are concerned with making meaning and children draw on existing knowledge in each mode for learning in the others.

- There is an important distinction between deciding what you want to say and actually writing it down, between the composing and the secretarial skills of writing. The secretarial skills – handwriting and spelling – are important, but composition is even more crucial.

- Writing is a social process. Frank Smith (1982), for instance, talks in terms of creating an atmosphere in schools and classrooms which is akin to a 'literacy club' which all children, when motivated by an enthusiastic adult, will want to join.

- Writing is a craft which involves a number of different stages, including drafting, revising and editing.

Becoming a writer

Children have to gain control over those aspects of the writing system which make speech visible: letters, words, punctuation and so on. But writing is much more than the transcription of speech, both in form and in function. Most speech takes place face to face: there is a great deal of repetition and redundancy and the listener has the opportunity to interrupt or seek clarification. Writing transforms ephemeral speech into a permanent record. It is expected to express 'complete thoughts' which can be understood by readers removed in time and space. And, because it can be read and reread, it is much less redundant and repetitious than speech.

The grammar and organization of speech and writing are also very different. While the basic unit in writing is the sentence, speech is organized in clauses. Similarly, children have to learn paragraphs, episodes and larger textual structures which don't exist in speech.

Various developmental stages can be detected along the road to competence in writing. In the very early stages, children experiment with making marks on paper, either to send messages or to imitate adults. This kind of writing is sometimes referred to as role play writing.

Role play writing in English and Chinese

Very soon role play writing gives way to experimental writing. Children begin to write in words, using some of the letters of conventional writing. They show an awareness of directionality and of the difference between letters and numbers. Children who have been exposed to different scripts are able to tell which is which. Viv Wheatley (1991), for instance, reports Amritpal's excited reaction on first seeing Panjabi appear on the VDU of the nursery computer: 'Gurdwara – it's in Gurdwara'. He was clearly relating the print on the screen to notices and books he had seen in the Sikh temple.

Children tend to focus in their early writing on subjects that are important to them, and they frequently return to similar themes, eg family, space creatures, dinosaurs and princesses. Although their writing tends to mirror speech quite closely, they have a clear sense of sentence and soon attempt to use some punctuation.

Early writing gradually gives way to conventional writing. Children are able to use writing for different purposes, such as stories, plays and reports. They use a range of compound, simple and extended sentences and can group related information into paragraphs. They punctuate simple sentences correctly and use a range of strategies for planning and revising their work. They are well on the road to becoming proficient writers.

Writing and culture

Many people take it for granted that children from working class or ethnic minority communities have very limited exposure to the written word. Such assumptions are without foundation. It is, however, true that who writes what, when and to whom can differ greatly from one community to another. Shirley Brice Heath (1983), for instance, describes how writing in Trackton, an African American community in the south east USA, is usually a female activity; most men write only for financial reasons: signatures on cheques, figures and notes for income tax returns. Women, on the other hand, use writing to remember important dates, phone numbers and addresses, and on greetings cards and absence notes for children. More extended writing, such as church bulletins and orders of service, is negotiated cooperatively at meetings: no one individual takes responsibility.

The literacy practices in Trackton are very different from those of Gujarati speaking Moslems and Hindus in Britain. Bhatt et al (1994) describe how Babhubhai and Yusufbhai have used letter writing throughout their lives as an important way of maintaining family bonds. Although the phone has taken over this function for family and friends close by, Babhubhai still writes to his sister in Gujarati and English, while Yusufbhai corresponds with friends overseas in Gujarati. As a prominent member of two Hindu organisations, Babhubhai writes speeches, the minutes of meetings and correspondence in Hindi, while Yusufbhai writes the notes in preparation for his meeting at the Ismaili place of worship in Gujarati.

It is important for teachers to be aware of different attitudes towards the written word. However, there is no simple equation between exposure to print and success in reading and writing. Urzúa (1986) makes this point very clearly in a comparison of three Cambodian refugee families. In Vuong's home, there was no shortage of reading materials: bus schedules, maps, calendars, newspapers, brochures and newsletters as well as a range of bilingual dictionaries were clearly on display. In contrast, Cham and Sonkla lived with their widowed mothers in apartments where there was very little evidence of reading material. The only visible materials were calendars, letters from relatives, the phone book and books from school.

Those who stress the value of children's early literacy experiences might expect Vuong to have made much more rapid progress than Cham and Sonkla. This was not the case. Vuong was struggling with literacy in a class where the teacher emphasized discrete skills, full group instruction, copying and filling blanks. Cham and Sonkla, in contrast, were in a class where the teacher placed emphasis on writing as a developmental process and on reading with meaning rather than on sub-skills. Both children were reading and writing enthusiastically.

The teaching of writing

Two approaches to the teaching of writing are particularly supportive of this integrated view of language skills. The first – language experience – is designed for use in the very early stages. The second – process writing – helps children develop more advanced writing skills.

Language experience

The language experience approach integrates all language skills: children discuss an experience with the teacher; they dictate a 'story' based on this discussion which the teacher writes down; they read and reread the finished story; they can then copy the story out themselves.

The most common commercial materials based on the language experience approach are Longman's *Breakthrough to Literacy*. Children take printed cards from a big board containing commonly used words and place them in a plastic stand. The teacher writes on card any words not included in the bank of common words. Children copy the story into their books.

As children's sight vocabulary grows, they are given a folder which is a smaller version of the big board. Later they work with a personal dictionary, set out in alphabetical order, where teachers write down the words they need for their stories.

The language experience approach has several advantages. The integration of the different language skills is very helpful: prior discussion serves as a valuable rehearsal of both the ideas and the vocabulary they will use in writing; and the fact that the story is based on children's own speech patterns increases their chance of success when they read.

Some teachers are unsure how to react when children's stories don't conform to conventional English patterns. Too much teacher intervention detracts from children's pleasure in making meaning. However, it is always possible to provide an accurate model in your response.

Process writing

Process writing has evolved largely as a result of the work of Graves (1983) and Calkins (1983) in the USA. In the UK, it was promoted through the National Writing Project and it also underpins the approach to writing recommended in the national curriculum for English.

Process writing takes place in classrooms where real writing is given a high priority, where children are given a range of reasons for writing and work in an·atmosphere which encourages collaboration and mutual support. There are six main steps:

- *Rehearsal* Before starting, children need to discuss the topic for writing as well as the details of what they are going to write.

- *Drafting* Children quickly write down their ideas, using invented spellings if they don't yet know the conventional ones.

- *Responding to writing* Children share their work in large groups, small groups or one to one with the teacher, receiving feedback and encouragement which helps them to revise their work.

- *Revision* Children use this feedback to reflect on their writing. Not all pieces of writing will be revised, only those which they have very much enjoyed or which may be destined for a particular audience. In responding to feedback, they may want to add more detail, delete words, sentences or sections, or reorder some parts. Teachers can demonstrate numbering systems for moving around or adding text, or how to cut and paste either by hand or using a wordprocessor.

Harriet uses numbers to show where new text should be inserted on Friday I went to London by my father and my Baradar. we went to the my father frand house . and looked at the veDy I liked . at hith we went to the Bagar I liked . we back to the my father frand house and I Paly games and we went back to Rading by train.

Shafti circles words she suspects are incorrectly spelled before consulting her teacher

- *Editing* When the writing is aimed at a particular audience, it is important that it follows the normal conventions of spelling and punctuation. When children are satisfied with the content of their work and are ready to edit, they can use symbols to indicate areas of concern before consulting the teacher.

- *Publishing* Not every piece of writing is suitable for publication but work which children have enjoyed and others will find interesting should be taken through the various stages of composition and transcription until it is ready to be 'published' in a form suitable for a wider audience.

Writing workshops

Process writing is sometimes organized into 'writing workshops' (cf Graves 1983; Gregory *et al* 1991). There are very specific guidelines as to how the workshops should be organised and how children can be inducted into the various routines. There is also a strong expectation that everyone takes part and, at the start of every workshop, not only the children but also the teacher should be involved in writing.

The structure offered by workshops not only promotes children's development as writers within a meaningful social context; it also offers certain organizational advantages. In more traditional teaching, the response to children's work comes at the end; in writing workshops, teachers are free to move around the room and offer support when it is needed.

Process writing – whether or not in the context of workshops – is supportive of the writing development of all children. However, it is particularly helpful in the case of bilingual children for two main reasons. First, the opportunity to rehearse ideas, vocabulary and structures provides a valuable boost to children's confidence. Second, this approach has the potential to reduce children's anxiety and to encourage risk taking. Because children are not expected to produce perfect copy at the first attempt, process writing can help alleviate the sense of failure which bilingual learners often feel when their writing is 'corrected'.

Rehearsal for writing

Whatever the reason for writing, children need plenty of opportunity to share ideas, to discuss what they are going to write about and how they will set about the task. This 'rehearsal' helps them to clarify what they want to say; it motivates them to write; and it provides the information, vocabulary, syntax and writing structures that they need. Various strategies can be used to provide both a stimulus and a structure for composition.

Group writing

Communal writing is an excellent way of modelling all aspects of the writing process. It allows children to develop ideas, strategies and style in the security of the group. It is particularly helpful for bilingual learners. Everyone can help to make decisions about how to start, which points to include, how much detail, which exact words should be used and what counts as a satisfactory ending.

It is important to model the entire process, from selecting the topic to the finished piece of writing. It is also important to model different kinds of writing: narrative, expository, poetry and so on.

Communal writing allows the teacher to demonstrate the craft of writing, complete with crossings out, additions, omissions, the search for the right word and authentic dialogue. Children learn from each other; they also learn by watching as the teacher writes.

With younger children or inexperienced writers, the teacher acts as scribe. With older children, a member of the group can perform this role. Children can also write in pairs or small groups, helping each other both to compose and transcribe their ideas.

A spread from a book produced by a group of 5–6 year olds with the teacher acting as scribe

This time the Romans thought they had trapped Hannibal in a narrow pass. But they hadn't! Hannibal's men set fire to bundles of twigs on the oxen's heads and pushed them past the Romans.
Through the smoke, the Romans thought Hannibal's men were trying to escape.
By the time they realised their mistake, Hannibal was miles away.

Poetry in Tower Hamlets

In the past, poetry was often perceived as a complex cultural form far removed from the everyday experience of children, particularly bilingual learners. Many teachers disagree, pointing to the rich poetic tradition which children from all cultures experience in the form of lullabies and nursery rhymes. This tradition is also evident in children's playground rhymes and clapping songs, in pop songs, advertising slogans and jingles.

Rhymes put across a number of important messages: word play can be fun; it is possible to break the rules of logic and common sense; rhythm and rhyme provide an important framework for writing.

Elena Mauro and Monica Forty (1994) describe a range of group writing possibilities in work on poetry with a class of seven year olds in Tower Hamlets where most of the children are Sylheti speakers from Bangladesh. They decided to build on children's knowledge of different poetic forms, and started by modelling different versions of *Twinkle, Twinkle Little Star*, such as:

> Twinkle twinkle little star
> Up there in the blue
> How I wonder who you are
> Are you Doctor Who?

The children chose a range of different colours to make their own rhymes and, with the teacher's help, were able to construct the sentences to fill the gaps

> Twinkle twinkle little star
> Up there in the ...
> How I wonder who you are
> ....

Twinkle twinkle little star
Up there in the green
How I wonder what you are
My favourite food is baked beans

Mahbuba, 7 years

In another activity, children composed poems about night. After looking at favourite pieces in English and Bengali, the teacher modelled how the children might set about writing a poem by asking questions like, 'Where are we?' and 'What can we hear?' The children agreed on a chorus, *In the night, in the night*, which they thought sounded 'creepy'.

They then worked in groups of three, organized according to their level of experience. Some worked with sheets where *In the night, in the night* was repeated several times, with spaces in between and prompts on how they should respond. Some were given a sheet with a set of speech bubbles containing the prompts 'I see,' 'I hear,' 'I feel' and blanks where they could write their response.

A small group of beginners in English were given a grid of eight boxes for drawing pictures. The teacher acted as scribe when the children described the pictures. Their responses showed they had understood the idea. For instance, Afsam wrote, 'Cat go miaow, ghost coming.' The teacher typed the poems and 'published' them in a book containing a contribution from all the children.

In the night, in the night
a dog saying woof
In the night, in the night
owl was going woooo!
In the night, in the night
I smell smelly socks
In the night, in the night
I feel scared
In the night, in the night
a ghost is coming
In the night, in the night
'Look, a witch is flying!'

Siddique, 7 years

Drama, puppetry and oral retellings

When children write plays to be read aloud or performed, there are many opportunities for extending their writing skills and reinforcing speech-print connections. Even beginners in English can take an active role in

9

productions of this kind and there are many opportunities for cooperative learning with native speakers.

The opportunity to retell familiar stories is also a valuable preparation for writing. Angela Henry and Mike Hill (1991), for instance, describe how children in a class of 10–12 year olds became interested in a collection of younger children's alternative versions of Cinderella. Their teacher invited them to tell each other stories they remembered from their own early childhood.

Anwara recognised Cinderella as a Bengali story and enlisted her teacher's help in tracking down all the versions of Cinderella in the school. Using her own resources, other children and adults, she set about writing her own version of the story. Other children retold, wrote and dramatized versions of the 'Three Little Pigs'. Given the opportunity to tell the story before writing, even previously reluctant writers took part enthusiastically.

Games to support writing

Sequencing activities provide a very useful framework for writing. The teacher helps children place picture cards – commercial or home made – in a sequence, then tell the story and write it. Children can also create their own picture cards for others to use. As well as providing scaffolding for writing, sequencing activities can be used as the basis for reading games and to reinforce language patterns: sentences can be sorted into a sequence, jumbled and reordered.

Games based around ' ideas cards' offer a variation on this theme. One pile of cards contains ideas for settings; another for characters; and a third for the problems or situations which they encounter. Children take a card from each pile and use this as the basis for their story.

Photocopied text cut into sections for children to reassemble and justify the order they choose

I could hardly wait for school to start

In the last week of the holiday

Neither could mum

I was feeling glum

10

Using the community language

The strategies outlined above are, of course, supportive of the writing development of all children. Whatever the stage of development of the children in question it is very important to provide an authentic stimulus which will engage their interest; it is also important to make the purpose of the writing task very clear.

Other strategies are open to teachers working with bilingual learners. There is every reason, for instance, to encourage beginners who are already literate to join in writing activities in the community language. Take the case of ten year old Shahed who came from Iran with a high level of literacy in Farsi but very little English.

In the early months, Shahed worked in Farsi while other members of the class were involved in writers' workshops. At the very beginning, his efforts were almost exclusively in Farsi, with just a short explanatory sentence in English and an illustration which helped explain what he had written to his teacher.

As his confidence grew, he moved to dual language stories, writing first in Farsi and then in English.

An early example of Shahed's writing

lamlike a micel jacson.

Writing in two languages: Farsi and English

I like my father and, He is very kind and my mother very kind and she is love me. my sisther is very good girl and she is kind. my mother is working in the university and my, father going to the libery and He is Riding the book and He like book, and He is artist and He talking to piupel.

END

By encouraging him to write in Farsi, his teacher was sending important messages to both Shahed and the other children in the class. She was making it clear that she respected his previous learning, the importance of maintaining his writing skills in Farsi, and the usefulness of these skills in supporting new learning. In doing this, she made it possible for Shahed to establish himself as a willing and able member of the class.

Shahed was, in fact, the only Farsi speaker in the class and, if his teacher had queries about his writing in Farsi, she liaised with his father. When several children speak the same language, however, there are more options. It is often possible, for instance, to enlist the help of others more experienced in English. Children who share the same language should always be allowed to do initial planning and discussion and, possibly, the first draft in their community language. Those already literate in the community language should be encourage to use bilingual dictionaries. Bilingual teachers and parents can also offer valuable support.

Concept keyboards

Information technology can also be a bridge to literacy in English. The concept – or touch sensitive – keyboard can be very useful with both very young children who have limited experience of the written word and with older beginners in English already literate in the community language.

The keyboard comes in two different sizes (A3 and A4), divided into 128 different segments. Each segment can be assigned its own function: a word, a sentence or a picture. Children press a key or combination of keys to produce words on the screen. Existing programs can be adapted for multilingual usage by adding overlays in other languages, although, in most cases, only the English appears on the screen.

Patricia Foster (1992) describes how she used overlays in English, Bengali and Panjabi for the Scenario *Moving in* program when working on household vocabulary with a mixed language group of recently arrived secondary school children. Even children with very little English could understand how to operate the program by reading the instructions in the community language. The overlays also had the effect of encouraging the children to use their first language when discussing what to do.

Alison Park (1992) describes how she used the Scenario *Elmtree Farm* program with ten year old Jaime, a boy who had just arrived in England from Spain. Working with him in a small group of children, she demonstrated how the package worked while another Spanish speaking child described the process in Spanish.

They used the overlays in several ways. While Jaime pressed the Spanish overlays, an English speaking child read out the English translation on the screen for him to repeat. Other members of the group gave feedback on his pronunciation. In time, the Spanish overlay was replaced first with the English version, then with a version where all the picture clues had been removed.

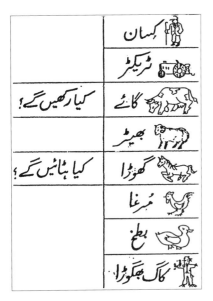

An overlay in Urdu to accompany the Scenario *Elmtree Farm* program

Reasons for writing

The normal school curriculum offers many opportunities for experimenting with different writing genres. Early efforts are likely to take the form of expressive writing which is close to every day speech, or poetic writing in the form of story and poetry. Children's repertoires gradually expand to include transactional or factual writing, eg lists, matrices and reports. Children also need real reasons and authentic audiences for their writing.

The activities described below are supportive of the development of all young writers; they have also been used with great success in multilingual classrooms which include children at all levels of development in English.

Writing and role play

The writing that young children do at home often has real intentions and purposes, arising out of everyday activities such as sending cards and letters, making lists or taking down phone messages. Writing in the early years at school often builds on these foundations: making posters and invitations for the the performance of a play, writing thank you letters and so on.

Role play is another rich source of real reasons for writing. Viv Wheatley (1991) describes work around a café in an infant school and nursery. There were many opportunities for writing, including taking down telephone messages, making menus, taking orders, and noting ingredients and recipes.

Children soon fell into role. Rajpal, for instance, went to the café office explaining, 'I must go and write what they want'. She read back her experimental writing to the chef and others as, 'Chips, beefburgers and ice-cream.' Later she wanted to write her order at the computer. She asked her teacher to point to the letters which she needed. Then she decided to 'write' by herself. She read back the order – rice, curry, peas – lengthening the vowels to make the spoken words match the print.

Helen Savva (1990) also describes role play around food. Following a visit to Soho, various props and artefacts were used to set up a Chinese restaurant in the corner of the nursery. Older children decorated the windows with Chinese writing and parents came to help cook Chinese recipes. Some of the children thought it would be a good idea to have a Chinese school. Some ten year olds were brought in three times a week to teach Chinese to an 'option group' of under fives.

The impact of this role play was unmistakable. Children were more willing to use their home language – both spoken and written – and to talk about their life outside school. Non-Chinese children have also benefited from this more open atmosphere. Monolingual children understand that other languages exist in spoken and in written form and other bilingual children are more confident about speaking and writing their own home languages.

Viv Wheatley also describes work around role play with slightly older-children, in this case a class of six and seven year olds at James Watt Infant School in Birmingham (Minns 1991). Following work on road safety, the children arrange a special area of the class set aside for role play as a police station. They sat at a phone ready to receive and write down emergency calls. They designed forms asking for details of name, address and date of birth. Soon they were weaving their stories in both Panjabi and English around their play.

Dialogue journals

In simple terms, a dialogue journal is a written conversation between a teacher and a student. Students write regularly about whatever they choose and for as long as they want. Teachers respond to the content: they don't 'correct' the writing or make evaluative comments like 'Well done!' or 'That was interesting'. Instead they write a genuine response to what the child has to say. Student and teacher make equal contributions, offering observations and opinions, asking and answering questions.

A page from ten year old Shadi's dialogue journal

Irahs. my school at home is called trah
Ther are 8 teachers and They are 156
childreh. the play ground is big and hice.
it has 4 trees. the classroom is big is has
besk sand chairs, pictures on the wall. It is
big and bedtiful. It is made of brick. 42 children
2 teachers.

Your school is much smaller than ours! Tell me about your special friend.

Her hame is mariam. she is a 8 years old.
she lives in t cheran. she is a good girl. she is tall
and thin She has blohde hair. She has black
eyes. she wears trousers she is in my clas
we go swimming. We go to school toge fher on
the bus

What a nice person. Do you miss her?

Dialogue journals can be used with children of all ages and at all levels of competence in English. Joy Kreeft Peyton and Leslie Reed (1990) suggest that, for children with no English and little experience of literacy, journals can start as interactive picture books. As children begin to learn to write letters and words, the teacher can start to label pictures or write brief descriptions or explanations below. Children not yet able to write independently who want to write rather than draw can dictate their entries. The teacher can ask children to talk about what they have drawn or written, helping them to extend their entries orally before writing her own response in their presence, reading as she writes.

When children are literate in another language and bilingual support teachers are available, there is no reason why the dialogue journal should not be written in the community language.

Dialogue journals offer many benefits for all children, including more advanced writers. They allow the teacher to tailor responses to the language needs of the child in question and offer very useful models in the target language. They give teachers and children the opportunity to get to know each other better. They can also accommodate personality differences. For instance, there are many cases of beginners who are willing to write in a dialogue journal well before they are able to talk in front of classmates.

When students write in dialogue journals they are obviously working on fluency not accuracy. In a situation where they know that writing won't be corrected, it is easier to take risks. These are precisely the conditions which need to be in place for children to develop as writers.

Written conversations on computer networks

Computer networks offer children exciting new possibilities for writing to and with other children – in other classes, in other parts of the country, and even in other countries. As well as exchanging personal information, there is the chance to work with other children on a range of projects. Children at two sites working together to produce a newspaper, for instance, will not only have the chance to write articles to be read by a much wider audience than usual, but will need to negotiate tasks and strategies.

Non-fiction

Because narrative is closer to speech, children usually find this kind of writing easier than description, argument and other kinds of non-narrative writing which are organized rather differently. A useful way of introducing non-narrative writing is through the use of lists, tables and other ways of organizing information and ideas.

When children are already literate in their community language, the skills required will be readily transferred to writing in English. Take ten year old Shahed's efforts at brainstorming magnetic and non-magnetic materials. He organizes his list in columns, starting in English, but transferring to Farsi when the strain becomes too great.

Shahed starts to brainstorm in English, then switches to Farsi

ruber magnet wood glass آمرسی خطاش	کاس تراش پرگار خودکار پلنت

Ticklists and matrices also make very small demands on children's skills in writing English. None the less, they allow the teacher to see very clearly whether children have understood the content of the lesson. They also serve as a valuable springboard for children's independent non-narrative writing.

Presenting information in the form of a matrix makes very few demands on writing skills in English, but allows children to demonstrate that they have understood

Vertebrates	Example	Warm/Cold Blooded	Suckles young	Eggs	Body covering
mammals	cat	warm	yes	no	furry
bird	thursh	cold	no	yes	feathers
reptiles	adder	cold	no	yes	dry scales
fish	herring	cold	no	yes	wet scales
amphibians	toad	cold	no	yes	smooth moist

Writing in other languages

Some teachers assume that their sole responsibility is for teaching children to read – and write – in English and that other languages have no part to play in this process. However, our understanding of the ways we learn has greatly expanded in recent years. It is much clearer now that the cognitive skills associated with literacy are not acquired separately in different languages. Learning which has taken place, for instance, in Panjabi is readily transferred to English or other language learning situations. Increasing numbers of teachers view opportunities for writing in other languages as an important way to consolidate and extend children's competencies, and not as an obstacle to acquiring skills in English.

Most children from minority backgrounds will come to school with an excellent receptive knowledge of community languages; many will also have well developed spoken skills. The development of reading and writing skills, however, is more problematic. It requires extended exposure to the written language and opportunities to experiment. Those children who achieve high standards have either been to school in the home country or receive considerable support from community schools, parents or both. Given the very real practical difficulties, the best that teachers can hope to achieve is an atmosphere which acknowledges and encourages children's efforts outside school.

Getting it right?

Monolingual teachers are often unsure as to how best to foster children's writing skills. They also express concern about their inability to help when children make mistakes. This worry is misplaced for two main reasons. First we need to remember that mistakes are a natural part of the learning process, irrespective of the language in question. Second, although children need corrective feedback, monolingual teachers are able to call upon a range of bilingual adults, such as support teachers and parents, for help. The need to show bilingual children that their efforts are valued, and to provide a range of reasons and audiences for writing in two languages, needs to take precedence over concerns about possible mistakes.

Children need the chance to develop as writers in both their languages. There are various possibilities: they can work on their own, in collaboration with more experienced peers or with the help of bilingual adults. They can write for many different reasons and audiences: short pieces for a classroom display, the school magazine or a collection of class stories on a similar theme; more extended writing to be 'published' in books for sharing with other children in the class or for wider distribution through the school library.

Different writing systems

Most children's first experience of writing is in the home. It usually centres around parents and older siblings. Many bilingual·children also attend community classes or, occasionally, have a private tutor. The acquisition

Hace dos años …
Le garçon a commencé à …

Latin scripts

αβγδεζηθικλμνξοπρστυφχψω

The Greek alphabet

سہیل کو بلا دو

The Nastaliq script used for Urdu runs from right to left

ਤਿੰਨ ਲੱਕੜੀਆਂ

The Gurmukhi script used for Panjabi hangs down from the line

A Chinese character
Beginners sometimes work with squares subdivided into nine smaller squares to help them with the correct proportions.

A child's attempt at Islamic calligraphy
'Catherine' in the Nastaliq script

of literacy in the community language, then, is a high status activity which some families pursue enthusiastically.

The presence of other scripts in the classroom offers many valuable opportunities for learning about different writing systems. The differences between English and other non-latin scripts are subtle: the number of letters can be smaller or larger: sometimes there are additional letters (eg β in German); more often there are extra diacritics or accents (eg *café, garçon* in French; *mañana* in Spanish).

Writing systems like Greek and Cyrillic are more challenging: the letters which they use are often very different, though there are also similarities which can be interesting to discuss.

Both Greek and Cyrillic are alphabetic systems, with clear letter-sound relationships. Urdu and Arabic scripts raise a host of rather different issues. Here we are dealing with a consonantal rather than alphabetic writing systems: the vowels are represented by diacritics or dots above or below the letters. The form of letters also varies according to whether they stand alone, in initial position, in final position or in the middle of a word. When children learn the Nastaliq script used for writing Urdu, they need to know not only the shape of the characters, but their correct position between the top and base lines.

In the writing systems used for the Indian languages, including Gujarati and Panjabi, the letters do not rest on a base line but hang from a top line. The characters in both languages represent syllables rather than individual sounds. Another feature of these languages is the large number of 'conjuncts' formed by the combination of two or more characters. The shape of the conjunct is usually related to the characters that are combined, though this relationship is not always easy to see.

Chinese offers yet another solution for making language visible. The writing system is logographic: each character or graph represents a word or part of a word. When children learn to write, they are taught first to use the various strokes (lines, sweeps, angles, hooks) and the basic sequence (left to right, top to bottom etc) for combining the strokes. Chinese characters are constructed within a notional square.

Children are often enthusiastic about the chance to learn other scripts. The Multilingual Resources for Children Project (1995), for instance, describes how interesting work on Islamic calligraphy grew out of a project on writing and communication undertaken by Elizabeth Pye with a class of 10–11 year olds at Redlands Primary School. As part of the project children were asked to design name plates using template with a repeating eight point star shape as a border. Non-Moslem children had been exposed to Islamic art through tiles and pictures of mosques. They had also coloured in Islamic patterns as part of their exploration of shape and space in maths. One of the children asked a Pakistani visitor to the class to write their name in Nastaliq script as the centre-point of their design. As the child traced over the pencilled writing, this first request was rapidly followed by others.

Wordprocessing in other languages

Word-processing in any language frees children from many of the anxieties of writing. Spelling mistakes can be corrected with a few keystrokes; whole sections can be cut and pasted with very little effort. When multilingual software is available, bilingual children can take advantage of these same benefits to develop their writing skills in the community language.

There is growing interest in the use of multilingual wordprocessing in schools. There are two main kinds of program: the first is dedicated to a particular language and, in the case of non-latin scripts, can be very expensive. Urdu programs, for instance, use contextual analysis to substitute the correct form of a character depending on its position in the word. The second option is multilingual software which allows English to appear in the same document as one or more additional languages.

One of the four Panjabi screens on Allwrite, the most common multilingual wordprocessing program in educational use

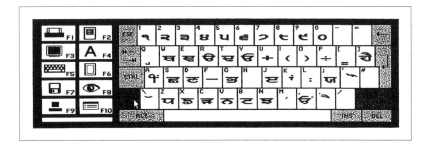

There have been a number of interesting initiatives to promote word-processing in other languages, including The Multilingual Word-processing Project (NCET 1992) and Parents, Allwrite and Languages (PAL) (Abbott 1994). It is easy to see why activities in this area attract a great deal of interest. Wordprocessing helps to raise the status of community languages. Shobhana Devani (1992), for instance, talks about the great excitement of children seeing Gujarati on the screen for the first time: 'Hey, look – my language is on the computer!' Gulshan Kayembe (1992) describes his own excitement on seeing ten year old Kalpana wordprocessing stories and poetry first in Gujarati and then, 'with an ease delightful to behold', providing an English translation.

Book making

Multilingual wordprocessing is a very valuable asset: it can be used for printing labels and children's names, as well as letters to parents. It can also be used for 'publishing' stories in other languages or as dual language texts.

These books can be written by both children and parents in collaboration with both monolingual and bilingual teachers. Shobhana Devani (1992) also describes how the presence of a multilingual word-processing package on the class computer encouraged Gujarati parents to come and dictate stories to the bilingual teacher which were then made into dual language bilingual story books.

Book making can also be promoted in classrooms where the teacher is monolingual. Penny Kenway (1994) tells how teachers in Wellington Primary School in west London set out to increase parent involvement through practical workshops, including one on writing stories for children.

One of the mothers who took part chose to describe the day she had gone with her daughter, Charlotte, on an outing with the nursery. By the end of the morning, she had written the script and typed it onto the computer. From then on she came in regularly to work on the illustrations with Charlotte and her special friend, Maheshi. Charlotte's mother asked Maheshi's father to translate the book into Sinhala.

This was not an isolated example. Other parents, either by themselves or in pairs, made translations of English story books in the nursery which were stuck above or below the English text with removable tape. These were used in class or at home by parents who could not read English.

The expert need not always be an adult. Shobhana Devani (1992) gives the example of a child who wrote beautiful stories in Gujarati which she then translated into English. She also became the scribe for other Gujarati speaking children who eagerly repeated stories they had been told by their parents and grandparents.

John Maxwell and Harbans Jassell (1992) describe how 11 and 12 year olds already competent in multilingual wordprocessing used this skill in making bilingual storybooks for younger children. Working in groups of three or four, they prepared the stories in rough and then redrafted as necessary. Next the books were translated. Wordprocessors were used to produce the final versions which the children also illustrated. As the teachers who oversaw this project commented: 'The children took great pride in this work and because they were able to leave their names as authors and illustrators on the books, it gave them a special sense of achievement.'

In all these cases, the presence of the wordprocessor was a very powerful catalyst for children's writing. However, wordprocessing is by no means the only option. Many handwritten books are equally effective

A page from *The hare and the tortoise*, a word processed dual language book produced by the Hounslow Language Service

સસલો ઝડપથી દોડવા લાગ્યો. આમબાને તેણે ઘણો પાછળ રહેવા દીધો.

Hare was very fast. He left Tortoise far behind.

Responding to writing

The old slap-on-the-fingers-if-your-modifiers-were-caught-dangling stuff …
Correct spelling, correct punctuation, correct grammar … hundreds of itsy-bitsy
rules … No one can remember all that stuff and concentrate on what [they] are trying to write about.

Zen and the art of motorcycle maintenance (Robert Pirsig 1974)

When children learn to write in a second language, they don't have to start
from first principles. Rather they use what they know in the first language
to hypothesize about writing in the second language. This knowledge
takes many different forms: how to make letters; which letters or combi-
nations of letters represent which sounds; the difference between speech
and writing; the processes and strategies involved in writing, and so on.

Exposure to English through all the language modes – speaking, listening, reading and writing – allows children to confirm or modify their
hypotheses as they go and provides a far more effective framework for
learning than, for instance, decontextualized exercises and drills.

Of much greater concern than departures from conventional spelling
and grammar is the fear of failure. Children who think their efforts will be
criticized or even greeted with ridicule are likely to respond either by
refusing to write, or by writing within a very narrow range. We make
progress as language learners when we feel free to experiment, when we
feel confident that our efforts will be received with interest and approval.

The teacher's response to children's 'errors' in writing is therefore criti-
cal. Perhaps the most constructive approach is to regard surface errors as
'slips of the pen'; they decrease significantly over time. Writing which is
exciting and sensitive to audience but which has 'surface' errors in
English should cause far less concern than writing which is technically
accurate but dull.

Focusing on the the content

The most important support that teachers can offer children is to respond
to the content of the writing. The child who writes *Mi bk st* needs more
attention to the missing bike than to the missing letters; the second language learner who writes *My father going to libery and He is riding the
book* needs a reply that focuses on his father. All work should be received
with pleasure and with interest.

Teachers should respond positively and in detail to the content. Writers
need to know what readers appreciate and why. What words or expres-
sions worked well? They also need specific feedback as to how they might
improve: is their story too long? Is there enough detail? Involving children
in assessing their own and other people's writing is also a valuable strate-
gy. By making response an integral part of the writing process, children
feel less fearful about making mistakes and more prepared to take risks.

The secretarial skills of writing

The realization that children need to develop different kinds of writing skills – composition as well as transcription – has proved invaluable in developing more effective approaches to the teaching of writing. While composition must always take precedence, teachers also have a responsibility to help children move gradually closer to conventional spellings and to develop a sense of the aesthetic in how they present their work.

Spelling

Learning how to spell in English is, by any standards, a difficult process. For various historical reasons, the sounds of the word are not a very reliable guide to how they should be written. Children with a good visual memory fare best: in their case, spelling is more likely to be 'caught' from reading than acquired through explicit teaching.

Spelling is very much a developmental process with children passing through various different stages on their way to becoming conventional spellers (Gentry 1987):

- *The pre-communicative stage* This is the equivalent to infants babbling as they learn to talk: children write down random letters to express meaning.

- *The semi-phonetic stage* Children attempt to represent letter sound correspondences, though very often important sounds are omitted, especially vowels, eg *dvd* for *David*.

- *The phonetic stage* All the sounds of the word are represented, eg *duz* for *does*.

- *The transitional stage* In due course, children start to pay more attention to visual patterns, making analogies with words they already know, eg *nea* for *knee*.

- *The mature stage* Children use their knowledge of word structure and can visualise the word in their mind's eye. Their spellings are correct.

As children develop as writers, it is very important to keep a sensible balance. Too much emphasis on spelling can detract from children's pleasure in writing but, on the other hand, too little emphasis at the appropriate time can stand in the way of progress. When more conventional spellers draw attention to their mistakes, or when others have difficulty in reading back what they have written, children's confidence can be seriously undermined.

Children need to develop explicit strategies for improving their spelling. Many traditional approaches have been shown to be ineffective: learning rules is of limited value because there are too many exceptions. Nor does giving children ready made lists of spelling have the desired effect. More successful approaches encourage children to focus on the appearance of words and common letter sequences (eg word families and roots). It is also important to train children to self-edit their work.

When bilingual learners are learning to spell in English, their efforts will be influenced by several different factors. Children's own pronunciation will often dominate when they are working on new words, where the pronunciation of English and the community language are close, or where an English letter or sound does not exist in the community language. Take the following example of writing from Abdul who had been learning English for a year at the time of writing.

Ten year old Abdul's story about his train set, written after twelve months of learning English

> I am wiating about my tarin sat
> I have a toy tarin it go's on a ryyl. it
> jo's very fast. it go's on elacture and
> it his batans and the butans can
> be control. olso you can control the
> tarin in any deracsan and olso
> you can put wood on top off the
> roof and it has a cemaney where
> the samke coms out. and runod
> the tarin there are plastc trees
> and plastc sattysun. dat all it has
> on my toy
>
> ABDUL

Abdul's writing clearly shows the influence of his home language: he puts a vowel between two consonants (*tarin* for *train*, *sattysun* for *station*, *samke* for *smoke*) because consonant clusters do not occur in Panjabi; and he makes more widespread use of a (*batans* for *buttons*, *sat* for *set*, *deracsan* for *direction*), again reflecting the sound system of Panjabi which has a smaller number of vowel phonemes. It is important to remember, though, that Abdul's writing contains many correctly spelled words, confirming that he is paying close attention to print. We need to recognize his creativity and problem solving abilities. He has made considerable progress since arriving in the country. Further exposure to English print, encouragement for his efforts and plenty of opportunities to continue writing will ensure that he works rapidly towards conventional spelling.

Handwriting

Children already literate in another language will be able to transfer their existing skills very rapidly to English, especially if they have previously used a Latin writing system. However, children with no previous experience of writing need to orchestrate an astonishing range of skills: holding the pencil, keeping the paper still, controlling their hand and arm, the direction of the writing, the shape, size and height of letters, and the spacing between letters and words. Infant teachers are already conversant with the different approaches to teaching handwriting; the teachers of older children may well want to refer to practical treatments of this subject by writers like Cripps & Cox (1989), Redfern (1993) and Sassoon (1990).

Children move through the same developmental stages in hand writing, irrespective of their age or which writing system they are using. They start with pretend writing in the form of a succession of marks on paper. They letter families

i l t u y j
r n m h b p k
c d g q o e
s f
v w x z

move from large, uncoordinated marks to shapes which resemble actual letters. As they learn to form the different letters or characters, and as their hand-eye coordination improves, their writing gradually becomes smaller.

Children with no previous experience, as well as those who have used a different writing system, need to be shown how to make the correct letter shape, and where to begin: it is helpful to explain that all letters in English start as the top except for d and e. Letters which are formed with the same basic movements should be taught in families.

The next stage is to encourage joining. Joins, as well as letters, should be taught in families, starting with letters that end of the baseline before moving on to top, cross bar and reverse joins.

i l t u h m n
a c d e k   o r v w   f t   a c d g o q

families of joins

baseline joins   top joins   cross bar joins   reverse joins

Mohammed learns to write

A clear developmental progression can be seen in the work of twelve year old Mohammed in his first months in his new country. Although he had never been to school before, he probably had some experience of Arabic, since he started copying words from right to left.

'a cotton reel machine' written right to left

e ʌ h ⊂ a ʍ ı e e ɣ ʌ o t t o ⊂ a

He found it difficult to hold a pencil and his fine motor skills were poor. At first his writing was barely legible and his attempts to draw round shapes in an exercise on area were uncoordinated. When he coloured in the shapes, he made large strokes which often went out-side the lines, just like a much younger child. He also enjoyed cutting out pictures and stick-ing them in his folders, but his use of scissors was very clumsy.

There was, however, an important difference between Mohammed and younger children: once shown how to colour more evenly, he immediate-ly adopted the new method. He retained new information very quickly and showed sustained concentration. Within four months he was able to write between the lines and distinguish between upper and lower case, though his words still tended to run into each other.

Do not use electric fires in the bathroom – Mohammed's writing four months after arriving in school

ᴅoʌo t ʋ ⊂ e ꞁ e ⊂ t ꞁ ⊂ f ı ꞁ e ş ꞁ ʌ t ʌ e b a t h ꞁ o o ʍ .

Assessment

Children's development as writers is multidimensional, encompassing both composition and transcription. As they progress, they show increasing control of the form and range of their writing. Their awareness of the needs of readers grows, as does their ability to undertake more extended writing. They gradually approximate to conventional spellings and punctuation and develop greater control of handwriting.

Development in writing is concerned with process and not content. This raises various issues for record-keeping and assessment. Because checklists and grids give only a very incomplete picture of children's progress, there has been a move towards writing profiles – longitudinal records which include samples of children's work covering narrative and non-narrative writing for a range of purposes and audiences.

The primary language record (Barrs *et al* 1988) offers a comprehensive approach to recording and assessing children's writing. It invites teachers to keep a diary of observations on children's writing in both English and community languages, focussing on issues such as interest and pleasure in writing; independence and confidence; evidence of experience with story and the conventions of stories; and understanding of written language conventions and the spelling system.

An extract from an observation diary recording development in writing

| 10th Sept. | Responded enthusiastically when I suggested he joined in writers' workshop in Portuguese. Obviously a confident and fluent writer. |
| 17th Sept. | Already adding English words to his writing in Portuguese so I can have a better idea of what he is saying. Dad came in this morning and translated some of his stories. Confirmed he is an avid writer at home. |

This cumulative record feeds into a termly assessment which is supplemented by an in depth look at particular pieces of children's writing. Teachers are required to provide a range of background information on each piece of writing (eg how the writing arose, whether the child was writing alone or with others, whether it is complete or an extract). They are also invited to record their own and the child's response to the piece of writing in question. Finally, teachers comment on the child's development of spelling and the conventions of writing, and on important changes since the last detailed look at a writing sample.

Although many teachers have complained that the approach taken by *The primary language record* is too time-consuming, it provides an excellent basic framework which teachers at both primary and secondary levels can adjust to their own individual needs.

Using the community language in assessment

Particularly in the early stages, it can be difficult to assess children's progress in writing in a second language. In certain situations, samples of writing in the community language can provide valuable insights. Ruth Cumming and Sheila Egan (1990), for instance, describe how Tripoon, an eleven year old Thai boy who had arrived some four months earlier, was reluctant to speak English. It was also difficult to gauge how much he understood.

Children in his class were doing research on animals found in the countryside: in Tripoon's case, this was the badger. He had learned some English as a foreign language in Thailand. However, he was much more confident about writing in his first language and so did his work in Thai. Piyachart, another Thai boy who had been in England for over a year, worked with him to produce an English translation.

This joint venture allowed his teachers to assess both his study skills and his understanding of content. His writing showed that he had understood the main features of the badger and had understood technical terms like 'nocturnal' and 'mammal'. He clearly had the ability to extract information from a text and synthesize this information in his own writing. The translation also gives an insight into Piyachart's bilingual skills.

One Thai child produced the first piece of writing; a second child with more experience of writing translated it.

แบดเจอร์

เป็นสัตว์ ที่ออกหากินกลางคืนอยู่ กันเป็นกลุ่ม
เป็น สัตว์ ชนิด ตัวใหญ่ เป็น สัตว์ ที่ ๑๖่ฬ แรง ๅๅๅม
ในหลุมที่ อยู่ใน ดิน เช่น, สัตว์ที่ดมกลิ่น อะไรได้
ออกๆ ลๆ ก ๑ปมี ตัวอาหาร ที่ มัน กิน คือ กระต่าย,หนอน,
ผลไม้, รังผึ้ง ทำความสะอาด ตัว เอง โดยขุด เปลือก
ไม้ ๑เสือ๑ๅ ตัวไป กู กับ เนื้อไม้จังใน

TRiPOOM   SUDT PiTUK

A badger is an animal that finds its food at night. It is a nocturnal animal. They live in big groups in a sett or an earth which they dig underground. It is a strong animal. Their eyesight is not very good, but their sense of smell and their hearing are very good. They have babies not eggs - they are mammals. They eat rabbits, worms fruit and bees' and wasps' nests. To clean the earth from their fur and claws, they rub against trees. They scratch the bark off the trees

References

Abbott, C. (1994) Supporting writing in community languages through the development and use of a multilingual wordprocessor, and the involvement of community groups and parents in its use. Paper given at the sixth conference on 'Computers and writing', University of Wales, Aberystwyth.

Barrs, M., Ellis, S., Hester, H. & Thomas, A. (1988) *The Primary language record.* London: Centre for Language in Primary Education.

Bhatt, A., Barton, D. & Martin-Jones, M. (1994) *Gujarati literacies in East Africa and Leicester.* Working paper 56. Centre for Language in Social Life, University of Lancaster.

Bissex, G. (1980) *GNYS at work: a child learns to read and write.* Cambridge, Mass: Harvard University Press.

Calkins, L. (1983) *Lessons from a child.* London: Heinemann.

Cumming, R. & Egan, S. (1990) Collaborative theme – related bilingual classwork at St Jude's First and Middle School, Portsmouth. *Languages matter* 3: 10–11.

Cripps, C. & Cox, R. (1989) *Joining the ABC.* Cambridge: Learning Development Aids.

Foster, P. (1992) Using mother-tongue on the concept keyboard in secondary schools. In NCET (1992), pp. 39–43.

Devani, S. (1992) The Gujarati Folio Project. In NCET (1992), pp 8–10.

Gentry, R. (1987) *SPEL ... is a four letter word.* Leamington Spa: Scholastic.

Graves, D. (1983) *Writing: teachers and children at work.* London: Heinemann.

Gregory, A., Redfern, A. & Lyons, H. (1991) *Writers' workshop: on becoming a writer.* Stoke-on-Trent: Trentham Books.

Heath, S.B. (1983) *Ways with words: language, life and work in communities and classrooms.* Cambridge: Cambridge University Press.

Henry, A. & Hill, M. (1991) Powerful stories. In Open University (1991) Milton Keynes: Open University.

Kayembe, G. (1990) Words of honour. *Times Educational Supplement* 21 September

Kenway, P. (1992) *Working with parents.* Reading: Reading and Language Information Centre, University of Reading.

Mauro, E. & Forty, M. (1994) Season of mists and Club biscuits. *Language and learning.* March/April: 9–13.

Maxwell, J. & Jassell, H. (1992) Bilingual story books in a middle school. In NCET (1992), pp. 49–53.

Minns, H. (1991) *Primary language: extending the curriculum with computers.* Coventry: National Council for Educational Technology.

Multilingual Resources for Children Project(1995) *Building bridges: multilingual resources for children.* Clevedon, Avon: Multilingual Matters.

National Council for Educational Technology (NCET)(1992) Look – my language is on the computer: Information Technology in the multilingual classroom. Unpublished manuscript, NCET, Coventry.

Park, A. (1992) Using bilingual overlays with the concept keyboard in the primary school. In NCET (1992), pp. 33–5.

Peyton, J. & Reed, L. (1990) *Dialogue journal writing with nonnative English speakers: a handbook for teachers.* Alexandria, Va: Teachers of English to Speakers of Other Languages.

Pirsig, R. (1974) *Zen and the art of motorcycle maintenance: an enquiry into values.* London: Bodley Head.

Redfern, A. (1994) *Handwriting skills.* Leamington Spa: Scholastic.

Sassoon, R. (1990) *Handwriting: the way to teach it.* Cheltenham: Stanley Thornes (Publishers) Ltd.

Savva, H. (1990) The rights of bilingual children. In R. Carter (ed.)(1990) *Knowledge about language and the curriculum.* Seven Oaks, Kent: Hodder & Stoughton, pp. 248–68.

Smith, F. (1982) *Writing and the writer.* London: Heinemann.

Urzúa, C. (1986) A children's story. In P. Rigg & D. Enright (eds) *Children and ESL: integrating perspectives.* Washington DC: TESOL, pp. 93–112.

Wheatley, V. (1991) Wordprocessing in a nursery school. In G. Keith (ed.) *Knowledge about language: ref lecting on learning with computers.* Coventry: National Council for Educational Technology.

Useful addresses

LETTS, John Ruskin Street, London SE5 0PQ
(tel 0171 587 1208)
Allwrite, multilingual wordprocessing package.

Northwest SEMERC, Fitton Hill CDC, Rosary Road, Oldham OL8 2QRE
(tel 0161 627 4469)
Scenario, What's that picture? Picture Store, and *Concept keyboard match,* all of which can be used with multilingual overlays for the Concept keyboard.

ESM, Duke Street, Wisbech, Cambridgeshire PE13 2AE
(tel 01945 63441)
Folio multilingual wordprocessing package and *Podd* for Concept keyboard.

Hounslow Language Service Hounslow Education Centre, Martindale Road, Hounslow TW4 7HE (tel 0181 570 4186)
Concept keyboard overlays for *Scenario* and *Podd* in Bengali, Chinese, Gujarati, Hindi, Panjabi, Urdu and Creole.